ATTORNEYS' VIEWS OF LOCAL RULES
LIMITING INTERROGATORIES

By John Shapard and Carroll Seron
Federal Judicial Center

1986

This paper is a product of a study undertaken in furtherance of the Center's statutory mission to conduct and stimulate research and development on matters of judicial administration. The analyses, conclusions, and points of view are those of the authors. This work has been reviewed by Center staff, and publication signifies that it is regarded as responsible and valuable. It should be emphasized, however, that on matters of policy the Center speaks only through its Board.

FJC-SP-86-1

TABLE OF CONTENTS

LIST OF TABLES

SUMMARY

This paper reports the results of a survey of practicing attorneys in twelve federal judicial districts concerning their experience with local district court rules limiting the number of interrogatories that one party may serve on another without leave of court to serve more. The survey was undertaken at the request of the Advisory Committee on Civil Rules of the Judicial Conference of the United States to help inform the committee's decision regarding proposals to impose similar limitations on a national level by amendment to the Federal Rules of Civil Procedure.

A survey questionnaire was sent to approximately four hundred attorneys from twelve of the forty federal judicial districts that have adopted local rules limiting use of interrogatories. Completed questionnaires were received from 271 attorneys.

Responses to questions about the effects of the local rules and about attorneys' attitudes toward them make clear that a majority of attorneys approves of the rules limiting use of interrogatories. Only a rather small minority opposes the rules. This majority approval is seen consistently among all identifiable subgroups of the respondent population: counsel from small, medium, and large courts; counsel involved in different types of cases, and counsel representing plaintiffs and defendants in those cases; and counsel with extensive experience in federal civil litigation as well as counsel with relatively limited experience.

There was a rather balanced split of opinion regarding the virtues of amending the Federal Rules of Civil Procedure. About 45 percent of the respondents opposed the imposition of limits by federal rule but supported continued authority to impose such limitations by local rule. Roughly 40 percent supported a federal-rule limitation. Another 10 percent thought there should be neither federal-rule limits nor authority to impose such limits by local rule. This pattern also holds consistent for nearly all identifiable subgroups of counsel.

The survey questionnaire also asked several questions relating to the use of interrogatories and requests for admission in specific cases the respondents had litigated in federal court. Responses to these questions suggest that requests for waiver of the limitation on interrogatories are rare, occurring in only about 6 percent of the 190 cases covered by the survey. The data do not show that the rules constrain the number of interrogatories served, because the reported numbers of interrogatories served by the respondents do not differ in accordance with differences in local-rule limitations. Despite this lack of apparent effect, more than one-third of the respondents indicated that the local rules led them to use alternative means of obtaining information.

These results are consistent with the view that the rules are effective in precluding unwarranted use of interrogatories without causing significant interference with the appropriate use of this discovery method.

I. INTRODUCTION

At the request of the Advisory Committee on Civil Rules of the Judicial Conference of the United States, the Research Division of the Federal Judicial Center undertook this study to ascertain attorneys' opinions about local rules of court that limit the number of interrogatories or requests for admission that one party may serve on another party without leave of court to serve more. The American College of Trial Lawyers, recommending that rule 33 be amended to limit the number of interrogatories to thirty subject to enlargement upon a showing of good cause, argued that such a rule would

> limit the number of interrogatories in the ordinary case while providing for more extensive use of that discovery mechanism under active judicial management when the nature and extent of the case warrants.[1]

The fact that forty federal district courts have by local rule imposed such limitations (see appendix A) suggests a fairly broad level of judicial support for this concept. Lacking any systematic information about how these rules are regarded by attorneys in cases subject to them, the Advisory Committee asked the Center's Research Division to conduct a survey of attorneys in districts with such a local rule. Pursuant to that request, approximately four hundred attorneys from twelve districts were surveyed in April 1985.

---

1. American College of Trial Lawyers, recommendations submitted to the Advisory Committee on Civil Rules (Apr. 9, 1984).

A local rule to limit interrogatories must seek to balance competing objectives. The point of such a rule is to limit excesses in the use of interrogatories. The lower the numerical limit, the more the rule will preclude service of unnecessary or unduly burdensome interrogatories. Whatever the limit, the court must provide for service of more interrogatories in cases where they are needed as a proper and efficient means of obtaining discoverable information, and the process of obtaining court permission to do so will necessarily place some burden on the parties and on the court. If this burden is too great, the rule may be counterproductive, causing problems greater than those it is intended to remedy. A limitation that is too low may create an intolerable burden from requests for waiver of the limitation. Excessive use of interrogatories can be controlled without imposing a numerical limit through the court's general power to oversee discovery and through an aggrieved litigant's option to seek protective orders and sanctions for discovery abuse. The implicit premise underlying imposition of a numerical limit must be that such a measure can control the problem more effectively or at less cost (or both) than the existing alternatives.

On the basis of the foregoing analysis, we reasoned that attorneys might oppose local rules limiting interrogatories if they thought that there had been no significant problem of excessive use of interrogatories prior to the adoption of the local rule (or that there would not be such a problem in the absence of the rule); that the procedures for requesting leave to serve more interrogatories were unduly burdensome; or that the limit was not low enough to correct the problem. Guided by these considerations, our study sought information about attorneys' perceptions of local rules limiting interrogatories and requests for admission, as well as their actual use of these methods of discovery.

II. METHODOLOGY

Two aspects of the study's methodology should be discussed: the selection of a sample of attorneys to receive questionnaires and the design of the questionnaire itself. Selection of the sample was a relatively complex part of the design, owing to our choice of objective and to practical constraints.

Our objective was not to provide a single, general description of the views of the average civil litigator toward rules limiting the use of interrogatories. Instead, we anticipated that the views of attorneys might vary from district to district because of differences in the rules or in districts' litigation "environment," so we designed the study to allow us to characterize the range of attitudes about these rules. With this in mind, we chose to select a sample of attorneys that would include reasonable numbers from districts with high, low, and mid-range numerical limits on service of interrogatories, and that would also represent districts of large, small, and medium size (as measured by the number of district judgeships allocated to the district). Table 1 identifies the forty districts with local rules limiting interrogatories, grouped by court size and limitation number.

We had no readily available list of names of attorneys likely to have had experience under the existing local rules. The only adequate source of such names was the docket sheets of civil cases filed in the district courts that have adopted such rules. Consequently, our sampling method required that we select a sample of cases (regarding which we had readily

TABLE 1

SIZE OF COURTS BY LIMITATION ON NUMBER OF INTERROGATORIES

Number of Interrogatories	Size of Court			
	Large (10+)	Medium (9-5)	Small (4-)	Total
20	N.D. Ill.	W.D. Tex.* E.D. Mo. W.D. Mo.	D. Alaska S.D. Ill.* M.D. Ga.	7
25	E.D. La.*	S.D. Cal. W.D. La.	S.D. Ga.	4
30	C.D. Cal.* S.D. Tex.*	S.D. Ind.* E.D. Va.* D. Md.	D. Kan. S.D. Miss.* N.D. Iowa S.D. Iowa* N.D. Okla. E.D. Okla. M.D. Tenn. W.D. Tenn. D. Hawaii W.D. Ky. D.N. Mar. I.	17
40	S.D. Fla.* N.D. Ga.		W.D. Va.	3
50		D. Minn.* S.D.S.C. M.D. Fla.	D. Del.* D. Neb. D. Wyo. D.N.M. M.D. Ga. N.D. Fla. N.D. Miss. M.D.N.C.	9
Total	6	11	23	40

*Indicates district selected for this study.

available information collected by the Administrative Office of the U.S. Courts), and then obtain the names and addresses of counsel from the docket cover sheets in the district courts.

The sample was selected as follows: We first chose twelve courts for participation in the study (the asterisks in table 1 identify the selected districts; table 2 provides more detailed information about the practice in those districts). The districts were grouped by size, with each group comprising four districts, one with a high numerical limit (forty or fifty), one with a low limit (twenty or twenty-five), and two with the mid-range and most common limit (thirty). For each group, we selected from computerized statistical data all civil cases disposed of in each district during the twelve-month period ending June 30, 1984.[2] To avoid selecting cases unlikely to have involved discovery, we excluded two types: those disposed of before an answer was filed and those having subject matter that rarely involves discovery.[3] The remaining cases were divided into two groups: those terminated before trial commenced and those terminated during or after trial. From each of these two groups we

---

2. These statistical records, compiled by the Statistical Analysis and Reports Division of the Administrative Office of the U.S. Courts, are routinely made available on an annual basis. Data for statistical year 1984 (July 1, 1983, to June 30, 1984) were the most recent available at the time the survey was conducted.

3. The following types of civil cases were removed: recovery of overpayments and enforcement of judgments ("nature-of-suit" code 150), recovery under Medicare (code 151), student loan (code 152), veterans' benefits (code 153), land condemnation (code 21X), foreclosure (code 210), all prisoner cases (codes 510 to 550), and all Social Security cases (codes 860 to 865).

TABLE 2

TYPES OF LIMITATIONS ON NUMBER OF INTERROGATORIES AND/OR REQUESTS FOR ADMISSION FOR SELECTED DISTRICTS

District	Interroga-tories Only	Separate Limi-tation on Each		Combined Limitation
		Interr.	Req.	
C.D. Cal.	30			
D. Del.		50	25	
S.D. Fla.	40			
S.D. Ill.	20			
S.D. Ind.				30
S.D. Iowa	30			
E.D. La.	25			
D. Minn.	50			
S.D. Miss.	30			
W.D. Tex.		20	10	
S.D. Tex.	30			
E.D. Va.	30			

randomly selected thirty-six cases.[4] The total target sample consisted of lead counsel for plaintiff and defendant in seventy-two case from each

---

4. We selected the separate groups of thirty-six cases to enhance the probability that we would obtain an adequate number of cases in which some discovery had taken place. The statistical records do not reveal whether discovery occurred. We reasoned that discovery was most likely among cases that had actually reached trial, but to minimize bias we did not restrict the sample to cases reaching trial, since fewer than 10 percent of all federal civil cases are actually disposed of in that manner.

four-district grouping--a total of 216 cases or 432 attorneys.[5] The total number of questionnaires actually reaching attorneys was about four hundred.[6]

In choosing the sample as we did, we recognized that it would be biased in two ways, and consequently would not yield questionnaire results that could be characterized as representative of the views of any easily definable population of attorneys. First, because we chose the sample from a list of cases rather than a list of attorneys, it tended to overrepresent the views of attorneys who appear frequently in cases of the kind included in the list. An attorney appearing in two cases in our list would have had twice the probability of receiving a questionnaire as an attorney who appeared in only one case. Second, the cases sampled did not represent equal "slices" from the caseloads of the twelve districts used in the study for two reasons. Because we selected an equal number of cases from each group of districts (large, medium, and small), our sample contained a higher percentage of each small district's cases than each large district's. Similarly, because we divided the list of cases into two groups--cases reaching trial and cases disposed of before trial--our

---

5. In cases involving more than two counsel of record, we selected for the survey the plaintiff and defense counsel whose names were listed first on the court's docket cover sheet.

6. We failed to reach all 432 attorneys potentially identified as lead counsel in the 216 cases for several reasons. We did not include the U.S. attorney as a questionnaire recipient in cases in which he or she was counsel of record (we did, however, include individually identified assistant U.S. attorneys). Similarly, we did not send a questionnaire when a law firm, rather than an individual, was identified as counsel. Finally, there were a few incorrect addresses and a few instances in which the attorney had died or had moved and left no forwarding address.

sample tended to overrepresent cases reaching trial, because such cases are less numerous than those disposed of before trial.

These biases in the sample were the understood and accepted consequences of our choice to limit the survey to a modest scale. Because of the biases, we cannot assume that the questionnaire responses, taken in the aggregate, are representative of any definable population of attorneys, but by making detailed comparisons of the responses of various groups of attorneys, we can draw reasonable conclusions regarding generally held views. As is shown in chapter 3, this survey provides clear and convincing evidence that attorneys generally support local rules limiting the use of interrogatories. Hence, our choice to minimize the scale of the survey and accept consequent methodological limitations has not impeded our ability to provide ample and reliable information to support resolution of the policy issues to which the survey was addressed.

A second element of the design of this study included the development of the questionnaire, which is reproduced in appendix B. Although it is in large measure self-explanatory, a brief overview may be useful.

Although the Advisory Committee asked us to survey the views of attorneys regarding these local rules, our sample selection procedure afforded an opportunity to obtain some descriptive information about the use of interrogatories and requests for admission in the cases identified in the sampling scheme. Parts 1 and 2 of the questionnaire contain questions that provide information about the use of interrogatories and requests for admission in these cases. These questions were included in the hope that they would provide evidence of the effects of the rules on the use of interrogatories.

Part 3 of the questionnaire asks about the respondents' opinions of their local rule and their recommendations for amending it, as well as their recommendations for modifying the federal rules to limit interrogatories or requests for admission.

Part 4 asks the respondents to provide basic information about the extent of their federal court experience. This question was included to provide a measure of the consequence of the sample's overrepresenting attorneys who appear frequently in civil cases. A bias of this kind is arguably desirable, since it has the effect of giving greater weight to the views of attorneys who have more experience with the rule than to the views of less experienced attorneys. We felt it important, however, to quantify the experience of the questionnaire's respondents in order to gauge the extent of this effect and to assess the possibility that the survey results might be dominated by the views of a small circle of frequent federal litigators.[7]

---

7. Table 12, in appendix C, demonstrates that the survey responses were not dominated by attorneys with extensive federal civil practices.

III. FINDINGS

Lawyers' Assessment of Local Rules Limiting Interrogatories

Of most immediate relevance to the Advisory Committee's request for this study are attorneys' views about the effectiveness of local rules limiting interrogatories. Tables 3 to 6 report various aspects of the respondents' opinions. Question 3A, set forth verbatim in table 3, asked respondents to indicate their assessment of the effects of the local rule. Seventy-three percent of those surveyed agreed that the local rule "exerts worthwhile control on . . . discovery," which we regarded as a clearly favorable assessment. Twenty percent indicated that the rule "encourages . . . less formal and less costly" means of obtaining information. (The respondents were invited to check one or more of the proffered assessments, so the percentages add to more than one hundred.) At the other end of the spectrum, notably fewer responses indicated negative assessments of the rules: that they lead to more costly discovery (15 percent) or generate time-consuming reworking of questions (11 percent). Similarly modest numbers of respondents indicated that the local rule does not make any difference; for instance, because "access to a protective order is adequate" (11 percent).

Question 3B (see table 4) asked what changes the respondents would suggest to improve their local rule. This question provided a more decisive vote of approval or disapproval. A majority of respondents (59 per-

11

TABLE 3

RESPONDENTS' ASSESSMENT OF THE EFFECTIVENESS
OF LOCAL RULES LIMITING THE NUMBER OF INTERROGATORIES[*]
(N = 271)

Answer	No.	%
It exerts worthwhile control on certain abusive, excessive, or simply pointless discovery	197	73
It forces use of other, more costly or less effective means of obtaining information	42	16
It encourages use of other, less formal and less costly means of obtaining information	55	20
It generates time consuming reworking of questions	31	11
It makes no difference:		
Doesn't solve the problem it addresses	18	7
There was no problem for it to address	10	4
Access to protective order is adequate	30	11
General court practices of overseeing discovery are sufficient control	24	9
It is not adequately enforced	5	2
Other	44	16

*The question was "Check one or more of the following statements that fairly describe your assessment of the effects of the local rule that limits interrogatories and/or requests for admission."

13

TABLE 4

RESPONDENTS' RECOMMENDATIONS FOR CHANGING
THEIR DISTRICTS' LOCAL RULES TO LIMIT INTERROGATORIES*

Answer	No.	%
Local rule is fine as is	159	59
Eliminate local rule	23	8
Should limit interrogatories and requests for admission to a combined total of _____	12	4
Should limit interrogatories to _____ and requests for admission to _____	22	8
Should limit interrogatories (only) to _____	18	7
Other	25	9
No response	12	4
Total	271	100

*The question was "Please indicate what changes you would suggest to improve the local rule in your district (place number limits in blank spaces)."

cent) indicated that the local rule was fine as it stood, while a distinct minority (8 percent) recommended its elimination. Between these extremes, there were some (28 percent) who recommended changes in the local rule.

Table 5 compares the incidence of support for these rules among various subgroups of the 271 respondents. The table uses three of the questionnaire responses as measures of support or opposition: whether the respondent indicated that the local rule "exerts worthwhile control over . . . discovery," and whether the respondent chose "local rule is fine as is" or "eliminate local rule" when asked what changes should be made to the rule. In every subgroup identified in table 5, at least a majority of respondents indicated support for the local rule. In no subgroup did more than 14 percent indicate that the local rule should be eliminated. This consistency of support across subgroups permits substantial confidence that the complex sampling procedure did not produce misleading results. There is little room for doubt that a majority of attorneys in the studied districts supports the local rules limiting interrogatories in those districts.

We also asked respondents to indicate their views regarding possible amendments to the Federal Rules of Civil Procedure that would impose limits on the number of interrogatories or requests for admission that one party may serve on another without obtaining leave of court. Table 6 reports the overall breakdown of responses. The pattern of opinions exhibits no majority view, but instead two widely held but opposing positions: 45 percent of the respondents opposed a federal-rule limitation, but favored retaining district courts' authority to impose limitations by local rule. Thirty-eight percent favored some form of federal-rule limitation. Comparison of answers to this question among different subgroups of respondents disclosed the same pattern of remarkable consistency as that exhibited in Table 5. The only comparisons that deviated more than a few points from this 45 percent to 38 percent "vote" were those between attorneys with greater or less experience in federal civil litigation and

TABLE 5

INCIDENCE OF APPROVAL OF LOCAL RULE BY COUNSEL, CONTROLLING FOR VARIOUS FACTORS

Response Group	Number in Group	Exerts Worthwhile Control	Local Rule Is Fine as Is	Eliminate Local Rule
Plaintiff's counsel	129	63%	58%	9%
Defendant's counsel	142	82%	59%	8%
Personal injury cases				
Plaintiff	36	72%	69%	3%
Defendant	51	76%	53%	10%
Contract cases				
Plaintiff	42	64%	57%	5%
Defendant	43	91%	70%	3%
Civil rights cases				
Plaintiff	29	59%	55%	14%
Defendant	30	80%	53%	7%
Size of district				
Large (10+ judges)	85	74%	54%	7%
Medium (5-9 judges)	101	73%	55%	11%
Small (1-4 judges)	85	71%	67%	7%
Limitation on interrogatories				
20 or 25	73	74%	56%	7%
30	165	70%	59%	10%
40 or 50	33	82%	61%	6%
Disposition				
Before trial	123	72%	63%	11%
After trial	148	73%	55%	6%
Number of federal civil cases counsel handled in past five years				
50 or more	85	79%	64%	6%
10 or less	77	74%	60%	8%
Interrogatories served or received in survey case				
Number served within 10 of limit	84	69%	51%	10%
Received more than served	52	79%	50%	4%
Served none	79	67%	56%	10%
Received none	91	74%	66%	10%

16

TABLE 6

RESPONDENTS' RECOMMENDATIONS FOR AMENDING FEDERAL RULES OF CIVIL PROCEDURE[*]

Answer	No.	%
There should be no uniform, federal limitation; local rules imposing such limitations should continue to be permitted	121	45
There should be no limitations imposed by federal rule, and local-rule limitations should be prohibited	30	11
There should be limits imposed by the federal rules, as follows:		
A limit of interrogatories only	45	17
A limit of requests for admission only	0	0
Separate limits of interrogatories and requests for admission	40	15
A combined limit on interrogatories and requests for admission	8	3
Other	12	4
No response	15	6
Total	271	100

*The question was "How, if at all, do you think the Federal Rules of Civil Procedure should be amended in respect to the imposition of limitations on the number of interrogatories or requests for admission that one party may serve on another without obtaining leave of court?"

In tabulating the answers, those respondents checking the answer "Same as in question B, preceding" (which pertained to the question set forth in table 4) were counted as having chosen the answer corresponding to that given for question B.

those between attorneys from different size courts. The data suggest that attorneys from small districts and those with less experience are more opposed to a federal limitation than are attorneys from large districts and those with more experience.

Only three of the twelve districts included in the survey impose limits on use of requests for admission. Because the questionnaire responses discussed so far were addressed to local rules limiting "interrogatories and/or requests for admission," it may be supposed that the level of support evident from tables 3 through 5 primarily reflects support for local rules limiting interrogatories. The survey results suggest that there is less support for limiting requests for admission. A number of respondents offered comments critical of the idea, saying that limiting requests for admission would be counterproductive. Among all respondents, only 19 percent directly indicated support for such a limitation.[8] In addition, attorneys from the districts that impose such limits were somewhat more critical of their local rules than were attorneys in the other nine districts. Only 46 percent indicated that the rule was "fine as is," and 16 percent advocated eliminating the rule. Only 27 percent supported imposition of any limitation by federal rule.

---

8. Accounting for the 19 percent were twenty-nine respondents from districts that do not limit requests for admission who suggested that their local rule be amended to impose such limits, and twenty-two attorneys from districts with such limitations who said either that their local rule was "fine as is" or that it should be amended in a way that would retain limits on requests for admission.

18

Findings from the Sampled Cases

The first page of the questionnaire had questions asking the respondent for information about the use of interrogatories and requests for admission in the specific case selected in the sampling process. The purpose of these questions was to determine whether the limitations imposed by local rule had any apparent influence on the conduct of discovery. Despite the fact that 231 respondents reported on discovery activity (pertaining to 166 cases), the data afford only very limited evidence that the rules have a tangible influence on the use of interrogatories.

The sole indication that the rules influence discovery is that 40 percent of the respondents providing information about discovery gave an affirmative answer to the question "Did you obtain information by other means (formal or informal) that you might have obtained by these devices in the absence of a local rule limiting them?" (The words "these devices" were to be understood in the context to refer to interrogatories or requests for admission.)

The questionnaire also asked the respondents to indicate the maximum number of interrogatories and requests for admission they had served on any opponent, and the maximum number served upon them by any opponent. If the rules limiting interrogatories had the effect of constraining the actual use of interrogatories, one possible manifestation of that effect would be that the number of interrogatories employed would vary in a systematic fashion according to the limitation number. Table 7 summarizes the reports of those attorneys who reported the number of interrogatories they served in the identified case. The percentages in the table total to one hundred in each column. The significant feature of

TABLE 7

NUMBER OF INTERROGATORIES SERVED AND PERCENTAGE DISTRIBUTION BY LIMITATION NUMBER

Number Served	Local Rule Limitation				
	20	25	30	40-50	Total
None	7	5	27	1	40
	27%	13%	21%	4%	18%
1-10	2	4	20	1	27
	8%	11%	16%	4%	12%
11-20	7	8	35	7	57
	27%	21%	28%	26%	26%
21-30	5	13	30	7	55
	19%	34%	24%	25%	25%
31-40	5	1	7	4	17
	19%	3%	6%	14%	8%
41-50	0	2	2	1	5
		5%	2%	4%	2%
51 or more	0	5	6	7	18
		13%	5%	25%	8%
Total	26	38	127	28	219
	100%	100%	100%	100%	100%

the table is that the percentages do not vary systematically or significantly (in light of the relatively small totals) as a function of the limitation number. For instance, roughly 30 percent of attorneys reporting any use of interrogatories reported serving a number between twenty-one and thirty, and the percentage does not vary in any convincing manner as a function of the local-rule limitation.

Forty attorneys reported serving more interrogatories than permitted by their local rule. Of these, only eight (20 percent) reported that they had sought court permission to serve more than the limit number.[9] It is unclear whether the low incidence of requests for waiver ought to be surprising. Among the local rules of the twelve districts included in the survey, only one specifically prohibits waiver of the limitation by stipulation of counsel. Whether the local rules are meant to permit such waivers or not, perhaps counsel simply disregard the local rule so long as the interrogatories are perceived as proper and reasonable.

If the local rules limiting interrogatories do have an effect, it may be simply that of deterring excesses without significantly affecting the use of interrogatories for proper purposes.

Other information about discovery activity in the sampled cases was reported by the respondents. Analysis of these data failed to provide any additional insight about the influence of rules limiting the use of interrogatories or requests for admission, but some of the data are none-

---

9. The high incidence of interrogatories exceeding the limitation is in part attributable to the presence in our sample of cases that had been filed prior to the effective date of the local-rule limitation (these represented about 20 percent of the cases in the sample). This was the result of our sampling from recently terminated cases, which was necessary to permit identification of cases in which discovery was likely to have occurred. We could not exclude cases filed prior to the date of the local-rule limitation without thereby biasing the sample so that it would include only cases disposed of relatively promptly after filing. Of the forty cases in which the number of interrogatories exceeded the local-rule limitation, only twenty-three were clearly subject to the rule. The remaining seventeen cases, filed before the effective date of the local rule, may or may not have been subject to the limitation when interrogatories were served. Even though we must remain uncertain about the precise frequency, it seems not uncommon that the local-rule limitations are exceeded, and more often than not without a request for waiver.

theless of interest, particularly as an aid in the design of future surveys of attorneys in federal civil cases; these data are tabulated, with brief commentary, in appendix C.

Comments by Respondents

The last part of the questionnaire solicited any additional comments the respondent chose to offer. One hundred respondents (37 percent) offered some comment. Many of the comments merely restated the views expressed in answer to questions concerning the local-rule limitations or possible amendments to the federal rules. Other comments that occurred with some frequency were as follows:

1. The limitation on the number of interrogatories penalizes counsel who draft questions carefully and so reveal clearly each discrete subpart. The limitations thus encourage lengthy, difficult-to-answer questions.

2. The limitation forces greater reliance on depositions, increasing litigation costs and placing plaintiffs of modest means at a severe disadvantage.

3. There should be greater use of rule 37 monetary sanctions against counsel, either in lieu of "arbitrary" limitations on interrogatories or to enforce the local-rule limitations.

4. There ought to be a simpler, less costly means of requesting waiver of the limits. It is too much to require motion, brief, and appearance in all cases.

5. The questionnaire is a good idea, but it should also have covered other aspects of discovery.

APPENDIX A:
SUMMARY OF LOCAL RULES TO LIMIT INTERROGATORIES
AND REQUESTS FOR ADMISSION

District	Local Rule	Date Adopted	Limitation Interr.	Limitation Requests
Alaska	General 8(c)	Dec. 1983	20	--
C.D. Cal.	8.2.1	Oct. 1983	30	--
S.D. Cal.	230-(1)	Apr. 1982	25	--[a]
D. Del.	4.1B	Mar. 1983	50	25[b]
M.D. Fla.	3.03(a)	July 1984	50	--
N.D. Fla.	7(c)	1984	50	--
S.D. Fla.	1015	Dec. 1982	40	--
M.D. Ga.	4(a)	June 1984	20	--
N.D. Ga.	225-2(a)	Jan. 1985	40	--
S.D. Ga.	7.4	Feb. 1984	25	--
D. Hawaii	230-1(a)	Jan. 1982	30	--
N.D. Ill.	9(g)	Mar. 1984	20	--
S.D. Ill.	15(a)	Sept. 1983	20	--[a]
S.D. Ind.	14(c)	Jan. 1983	30	--
N.D. Iowa	2.3(.32)	Nov. 1983	30	--
S.D. Iowa	2.3(.32)	Nov. 1983	30	--
D. Kan.	17.d	Apr. 1984	30	--
W.D. Ky.	11(c)	Oct. 1980	30	30
E.D. La.	7A	Sept. 1982	25	--
W.D. La.	10-1-(a)(1)	Jan. 1983	25	--
D. Md.	6(B)	Mar. 1984	30	--
D. Minn.	3B	Jan. 1979	50	--
N.D. Miss.	c-12(a)	May 1978	50	--
S.D. Miss.	17	May 1980	30	--
E.D. Mo.	8	Oct. 1978	20	--
W.D. Mo.	15K	Jan. 1983	20	--
D. Neb.	9c	Sept. 1983	50	--
M.D.N.C.	205(b)	Jan. 1985	50	--
D.N.M.	10e	Nov. 1984	50	--
D. N. Mar. I.	230-1	May 1984	30	--
E.D. Okla.	10(d)	Mar. 1984	30	--
N.D. Okla.	10(d)	Oct. 1982	30	--
D.S.C.	order	Jan. 1979	50	20
M.D. Tenn.	9(a)(2)	Sept. 1982	30	--
W.D. Tenn.	9(c)	Sept. 1981	30	--
S.D. Tex.	10E(4)	July 1983	30	--
W.D. Tex.	300-6(f)	Dec. 1983	20	10
E.D. Va.	11.1(A)	Jan. 1980	30	--[a]
W.D. Va.	2.08(h)	June 1985	40	--
D. Wyo.	1(f)	Jan. 1980	50	--

[a] Local rule applies to a combined limitation on interrogatories and requests for admission.

[b] Local rule was amended during study and did not include limitation on requests for admission applicable to cases in the sample.

APPENDIX B:
SAMPLE QUESTIONNAIRE FORM

RE: Doe v. Roe, Docket # 83-01234, Northern District of State
Counsel for Plaintiff

Questionnaire on Rules Limiting the Use of Interrogatories

PART 1 Discovery Initiated on Your Part (if there was no discovery in this case, check here __ and skip to Part 3).

    A. How many interrogatories did you serve in this case (if multiple parties, maximum served on a single opponent)? Circle:

      0   1-10   11-20   21-30   31-40   41-50   51 or more

    B. How many requests for admission (if multiple parties, maximum served on a single opponent)?

      0   1-10   11-20   21-30   31-40   41-50   51 or more

    C. Did you request waiver of the limit on interrogatories or requests for admission?

            __No __Yes --- If yes, was it __granted or __denied?

    D. Did you obtain information by other means (formal or informal), that you might have obtained by these devices in the absence of a local rule limiting them?   ___No   ___Yes

    E. Please check the phrase that best describes the degree of cooperation between counsel in discovery activity in this case.

  __Cooperative __Slightly Contentious __Quite Contentious __Bitter

PART 2 Discovery Initiated by Opponent(s)

    A. How many interrogatories did your opponent serve on you in this case (if multiple parties, maximum by any single opponent)?

      0   1-10   11-20   21-30   31-40   41-50   51 or more

    B. How many requests for admission (if multiple parties, maximum by any single opponent)?

      0   1-10   11-20   21-30   31-40   41-50   51 or more

    C. Did opposing counsel request waiver of the limit on interrogatories or requests for admission?

            __No __Yes --- If yes, was it __granted or __denied?

PART 3 Your Opinions

A. Check one or more of the following statements that fairly describe your assessment of the effects of the local rule that limits interrogatories and/or requests for admission.

___ It exerts worthwhile control on certain abusive, excessive, or simply pointless discovery

___ It forces use of other, more costly or less effective means of obtaining information

___ It encourages use of other, less formal and less costly means of obtaining information

___ It generates time consuming reworking of questions

It makes no difference: ___ Doesn't solve the problem it addresses

___ There was no problem for it to address

___ Access to protective order is adequate

___ General court practices of overseeing discovery are sufficient control

___ It is not adequately enforced

Other: _____

_____

_____

B. Please indicate what changes you would suggest to improve the local rule in your district (place number limits in blank spaces).

___ Local rule is fine as is

___ Eliminate local rule

___ Should limit interrogatories and requests for admission to a combined total of _____

___ Should limit interrogatories to _____ and requests for admission to _____

___ Should limit interrogatories (only) to _____

___ Other: _____

_____

C. How, if at all, do you think the Federal Rules of Civil Procedure should be amended in respect to the imposition of limitations on the number of interrogatories or requests for admission that one party may serve on another without obtaining leave of court?

__ There should be no uniform, federal limitation; local rules imposing such limitations should continue to be permitted

__ There should be no limitations imposed by federal rule, and local rule limitations should be prohibited

There should be limits imposed by the federal rules, as follows:

__ Same as indicated in question B, preceding

__ A limit of ___ interrogatories only

__ A limit of ___ requests for admission only

__ Separate limits of ___ interrogatories and ___ requests for admission

__ A combined limit of ___ interrogatories and requests for admission

__ Other: _____

_____

_____

PART 4   Extent of Your Federal Civil Practice

Approximately how many civil cases have you handled in federal court, in which you had significant involvement in discovery:

In the last five years? _____   In 1984? _____

PART 5   We will be grateful for any comments you care to offer, about the subject matter of this questionnaire or the questionnaire itself

_____

_____

_____

_____

_____

THANK YOU FOR YOUR TIME AND COOPERATION.
PLEASE RETURN THE QUESTIONNAIRE IN THE ENVELOPE PROVIDED.

APPENDIX C:
SUPPLEMENTAL TABULATIONS OF QUESTIONNAIRE RESPONSES

This appendix provides information on those of the questionnaire data that failed to provide significant insight into the effects of local rules limiting interrogatories or requests for admission. Certain of these data will be of methodological interest, particularly to those planning future surveys of counsel in federal civil cases.

Use of Interrogatories and Requests for Admission

The following three tables account only for those respondents who provided an answer to the question tabulated.

TABLE 8

REPORTED USE OF REQUESTS FOR ADMISSION BY RESPONDENTS

(derived from question 1 B)

No. Served	No. of Respondents	% of Total
None	162	72
1-10	25	11
11-20	22	10
21-30	10	4
31-40	3	1
41-50	0	0
51-up	4	2
Total	226	100

27

TABLE 9

REPORTED NUMBER OF INTERROGATORIES SERVED UPON RESPONDENTS

(derived from question 2-A)

No. Served	No. of Respondents	% of Total
None	55	25
1-10	36	16
11-20	42	19
21-30	46	21
31-40	23	10
41-50	4	2
51-up	15	7
Total	221	100

TABLE 10

REPORTED NUMBER OF REQUESTS FOR ADMISSION SERVED UPON RESPONDENTS

(derived from question 2-B)

No. Served	No. of Respondents	% of Total
None	157	71
1-10	35	16
11-20	14	6
21-30	8	4
31-40	3	1
41-50	1	0
51-up	4	2
Total	222	100

Cooperativeness of Discovery

TABLE 11

DEGREE OF COOPERATION BETWEEN COUNSEL IN DISCOVERY

(derived from question 1-E)

Indication	No. of Respondents	% of Total
Cooperative	145	67
Slightly contentious	45	21
Quite contentious	21	10
Bitter	5	2
Total	216	100

Extent of Respondents' Experience in Federal Civil Litigation

TABLE 12

NUMBER OF CIVIL CASES IN FEDERAL COURT IN WHICH RESPONDENT HAD SIGNIFICANT INVOLVEMENT IN DISCOVERY

(derived from question 4)

	In Past Five Years (251 responses)	In Past Year (237 responses)
25% Less than	10	3
25% Between	10 and 20	3 and 5
25% Between	20 and 50	5 and 12
25% More than	50	12

Table 12 reveals a very broad range of reported experience of counsel. A substantial number reported very frequent litigation activity. Forty-seven respondents reported involvement in discovery of one hundred or more cases in the past five years, but twenty-three of these were from the Eastern District of Louisiana (and nineteen of these were involved in marine personal injury or marine contract cases). These twenty-three account for more than half of the respondents from that district. Ignoring the reports of counsel from this district, however, does not significantly alter the table, owing to a high incidence of counsel reporting at least fifty in the last five years. Even when we exclude counsel from Eastern Louisiana, 11 percent of counsel reported involvement in one hundred or more cases. Counsel with this extent of experience had a far greater chance of receiving our questionnaire than did counsel with, for instance, fewer than ten cases in the last five years. It appears, therefore, that there is a small cadre of attorneys who are very frequent federal litigators (the 11 percent mentioned above are not predominantly from U.S. attorney's offices). But the vast majority of counsel who appear at all in federal civil cases do so relatively infrequently.

Reliability of Responses

For eighty-one of the cases identified in our sampling procedure, we received completed questionnaires from counsel for both plaintiff and defendant. These paired responses afford a limited basis for assessing the reliability of the questionnaire data as measures of objective events in these cases, and for comparing counsel's assessments of the degree of cooperation between counsel in discovery. At least thirty-six of the eighty-one pairs, however, were associated with cases in which there were more than two parties (as indicated by the presence of "et al." in the case caption). (It is noteworthy in itself that about 38 percent of the 189 cases for which we received a questionnaire had at least three parties.) In these thirty-six cases, we could not assume that the discovery about which plaintiff's counsel had reported was necessarily the same

discovery as that about which defendant's counsel provided information.[*]
Hence we have forty-five cases in which we obtained two views that we
can presume are of the same events.

There are three bases upon which we can compare counsel's responses: the number of interrogatories served by each party, the number
of requests for admission, and counsel's characterizations of the extent of
cooperation in discovery. Table 13 summarizes the comparisons, showing
the percentage of paired reports that differ by a "factor" level. In the
case of number of interrogatories or requests for admission, a factor is a
difference in the reported range of figures within which the number falls.
There were seven possible answers: 0, 1-10, 11-20, 21-30, 31-40, 41-50,
and 50 or more, which we coded as 0, 1, 2, 3, 4, 5, and 6, respectively.
The factor differences are absolute differences in these coded values.
For counsel's assessments of the cooperativeness of discovery, the factors
are differences in the coded values 1 through 4 for the responses "co-
operative," "slightly contentious," "quite contentious," and "bitter."

---

*The questionnaire asked the respondent to report the largest
number of interrogatories served upon, or received from, any single
opponent. In cases involving a party other than the two from whom we
received questionnaires, the reports of the respondents might pertain to
interrogatories served upon or received from the third party.

TABLE 13

COMPARISON OF PLAINTIFF'S AND DEFENSE COUNSEL'S RESPONSES ABOUT THE SAME ASPECT OF THE SAMPLED CASE

Aspect of Case	Percentage Differing by a Factor of:					
	0	1	2	3	4	5
Number of interrogatories served by one party on the other:	33	37	11	15	4	1
Number of requests for admission served by one party on the other:	59	22	8	7	4	
Cooperativeness of discovery:	58	37	5			

www.ingramcontent.com/pod-product-compliance
Lightning Source LLC
Chambersburg PA
CBHW081312180526
45170CB00007B/2680